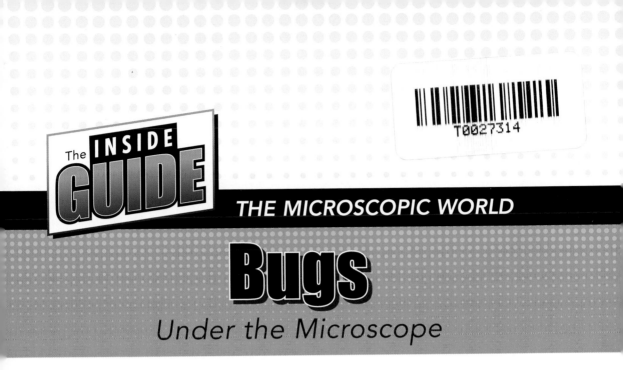

The INSIDE GUIDE

THE MICROSCOPIC WORLD

Bugs

Under the Microscope

By Sophie Washburne

Cavendish
Square

Published in 2024 by Cavendish Square Publishing, LLC
2544 Clinton Street, Buffalo, NY 14224

Website: cavendishsq.com

This publication represents the opinions and views of the author based on their personal experience, knowledge, and research. The information in this book serves as a general guide only. The author and publisher have used their best efforts in preparing this book and disclaim liability rising directly or indirectly from the use and application of this book.

Disclaimer: Portions of this work were originally authored by Janey Levy and published as *Tiny Bugs Up Close* (Under the Microscope). All new material this edition authored by Sophie Washburne.

All websites were available and accurate when this book was sent to press.

Library of Congress Cataloging-in-Publication Data

Names: Washburne, Sophie, author.
Title: Bugs under the microscope / Sophie Washburne.
Description: Buffalo, NY : Cavendish Square Publishing, [2024] | Series:
The inside guide: the microscopic world | Includes index.
Identifiers: LCCN 2022053991 | ISBN 9781502667908 (library binding) | ISBN
9781502667892 (paperback) | ISBN 9781502667915 (ebook)
Subjects: LCSH: Insects–Juvenile literature. | Microscopy–Juvenile
literature.
Classification: LCC QL467.2 .W372 2024 | DDC 595.7–dc23/eng/20221122
LC record available at https://lccn.loc.gov/2022053991

Editor: Jennifer Lombardo
Copyeditor: Danielle Haynes
Designer: Deanna Paternostro

Some of the images in this book illustrate individuals who are models. The depictions do not imply actual situations or events.

CPSIA compliance information: Batch #CSCSQ24: For further information contact Cavendish Square Publishing LLC at 1-877-980-4450.

Printed in the United States of America

Find us on

CONTENTS

Many bugs, including these firebugs, live in large groups called colonies.

SO MANY BUGS!

Chapter One

Bugs can be found everywhere on the planet. They live in tropical rainforests and dry deserts. They live in polar regions, on glaciers, and in caves deep in the earth. You can find them in cold mountain streams and in hot springs. Some even live in pools of raw petroleum, or oil, where they eat other insects that fall in.

Scientists have identified more than 1.5 million species, or kinds, of animals. About 1 million of these are insects, and scientists discover thousands more species every year. Some believe there could be more than 10 million insect species. When people think of bugs, they often picture creatures such as bumblebees, grasshoppers, butterflies, and spiders. However, most insects are less than 0.25 inch (6.4 millimeters) long. The smallest bugs are difficult to see without a microscope, but they can have a big effect on our lives.

Fast Fact

There are only a few kinds of bugs in Antarctica. One is called a springtail. It's also known as a snow flea because it lives in the snow and jumps like a flea. It isn't a true flea, though.

What Is a Bug?

Most people—even scientists who study insects and other small creatures—call any kind of small

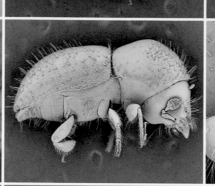
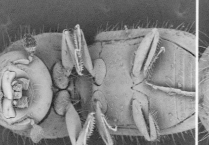

These photos show a bark beetle under a microscope. This kind of bug is smaller than a person's fingertip.

animal a "bug." However, there's a scientific definition for the word "bug." It's an insect that belongs to the order *Hemiptera*. These bugs don't have teeth. Instead, they have a mouthpiece called a

Fast Fact

Because people use the word "bug" to talk about things that aren't really bugs, insects that belong to the order *Hemiptera* are sometimes called "true bugs."

stylet that's shaped like a straw. They use this to suck the juices from plants or other small animals. Most don't feed on humans, although some will bite people if they get too close. They also have compound eyes, which means their eyes are made up of thousands of tiny lenses. Humans have simple eyes, which means we have only one lens in each eye.

Even on larger bugs, a microscope can reveal important details, such as a moth's compound eyes.

A FAKE FLY

There are a lot of animals whose common name is different than their scientific name. One of these is called the fairyfly. It's one of the smallest insects in the world—only about 0.005 inch (0.127 mm) long. That means it's small enough to pass through the eye of a needle!

There are more than 1,400 species of fairyflies, which aren't really flies. They're **parasitic** wasps that lay their eggs inside other insects' eggs. When the wasp larvae hatch, they eat the host insect still growing in its egg!

True bugs get their order name from the style of their **forewings**. For some bugs in this order, half of the wing is covered in a hard material called chitin. The other half is made of a **membrane** like other bugs' wings. This makes the forewings look like only half of a wing. "Hemi" is the Greek word for "half," and "ptera" is the word for "wings."

Many people—even some scientists—use the word "bug" to talk about any small creature with more than four legs. This includes spiders, ticks, and mites. These animals are arachnids, not insects. Insects have an **exoskeleton**, three main body parts, six legs, and antennae, or feelers. Most have wings, too. Arachnids also have an exoskeleton, but they have two main body parts, eight legs, and no antennae or wings. About 90,000 arachnid species exist worldwide.

Cicadas are one of the 40,000 species of true bugs in the world.

Many people don't like bugs. They're afraid of them or find them gross. However, some bugs are helpful to humans. For example, house spiders eat bugs such as cockroaches, moths, and fruit flies, which can cause big problems inside a home.

Fast Fact

Insects and arachnids have been on Earth for about 400 million years. They were here long before the dinosaurs!

Holes such as these in clothing are often caused by moths eating through wool and other fabrics.

OUT FOR BLOOD

About 14,000 species of insects feed on blood, but only a few hundred of those species target humans. Still, that seems like a lot when you're covered in bites! That also doesn't count other kinds of bugs, such as ticks and bed bugs. Bloodsucking bugs can be annoying and sometimes dangerous, because they can spread disease from person to person. However, looking at these creatures under a microscope reveals some amazing things.

Magnified Mosquitoes

One of the most common pests is the mosquito. Worldwide, more than 3,000 mosquito species exist. Most are only about 0.25 inch (6.4 mm) long. In the best cases, their bite is a little itchy for a few days. In the worst cases, they can transmit diseases such as malaria, yellow fever, and West Nile virus. These diseases can kill a person.

Mosquitoes are very small, so scientists need to look at them under a microscope to

Fast Fact

Only female mosquitoes bite, and the blood they drink isn't food for them. They need it to help the eggs inside their body develop. Food for adult mosquitoes comes from plant juices.

Mosquitoes breed in stagnant water. Drying out places where water collects after it rains can keep their numbers down.

Fast Fact

Mosquitoes have many ways of finding their food. Their antennae can detect the gas animals breathe out, called carbon dioxide, from 164 feet (50 meters) away. They can also detect body heat.

see the details of their bodies. Most mosquitoes are black, brown, gray, or tan, although a few are bright blue or green. Thin scales and fine, threadlike structures cover the mosquito's body and wings. Veins carry blood to the thin wings and stiffen and support them. Holes called spiracles run along the sides of the body and allow the mosquito to breathe. A pair of claws on each leg lets the mosquito cling to flat surfaces.

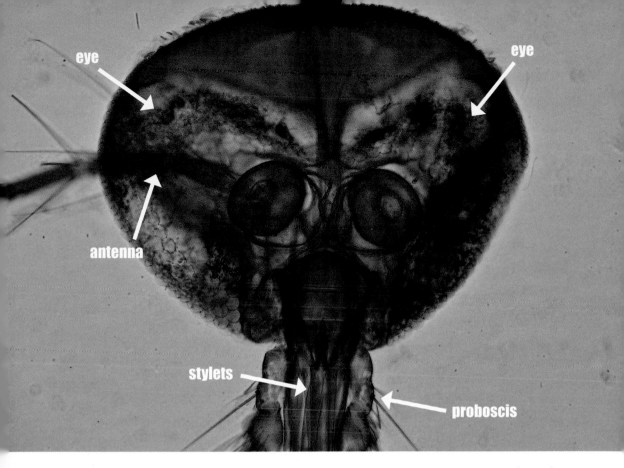

eye

eye

antenna

stylets

proboscis

This picture of a female mosquito shows what the parts that make up its head look like.

A mosquito's head is **fascinating** up close. Two huge compound eyes cover most of it. Between the eyes are two antennae, which the insect uses to hear and smell. A mosquito's mouth is funnel-shaped and doesn't have jaws. That means a female mosquito can't really bite its victims. Instead, it pierces the skin using a tube-like part called the proboscis that extends down from the mouth. The proboscis is made up of six stylets. Mosquito saliva, or spit, flows into the wound to keep the blood from clotting. The body's reaction to the saliva is what causes mosquito bites to itch later. Then, the insect uses its proboscis like a straw to suck up blood!

DISEASE-SPREADING TICKS

Ticks are bloodsucking bugs that are often found on animals and humans who have been out in nature, especially in wooded areas. Some kinds of ticks can spread diseases that can seriously harm a person. One of these diseases is called Lyme disease. This causes a rash and a fever. Over time, if a person doesn't get medical help, it can affect the heart and immune system.

The bite of the lone star tick can also sometimes cause a serious allergic reaction to a type of sugar found in meat and dairy products. People who develop this allergy can get sick or even die if they eat a hamburger or drink a glass of milk.

Deadly Fleas

About 2,500 flea species exist around the world. Females are less than 0.125 inch (3 mm) long. Males are even smaller— less than 0.04 inch (1 mm) long. If you see a flea at all, it just looks like a dark speck. They don't live on humans, but they will bite humans. Their bites are very itchy, and fleas can transmit diseases.

Fast Fact

Unlike most insects, fleas are wingless. They make up for this with their jumping skills. Their back legs are enlarged and have special stretchy pads to aid jumping. They can leap up to 13 inches (33 centimeters)— more than 100 times the length of their body!

The flea's mouthparts, which are called laciniae, can be seen in this picture. Laciniae cut through the skin and a needlelike part called the epipharynx stabs the blood vessel. Then, pumps in the flea's mouth and gut go to work to suck in the blood.

Under a microscope, we can see that a flea's body is flat from side to side to make it easy to move through an animal's fur or feathers. Long claws on their legs also help them move around. Hairs and spines on their body and head help them stay in place even when an animal tries to groom them off. Like a mosquito, the mouth is made for piercing skin and drinking blood. Each flea consumes 15 times its weight in blood each day!

When bugs eat our food, there's less to go around for humans.

Chapter Three

TINY PESTS

Many bugs are pests to humans. In most cases, bugs aren't trying to hurt us. They're just looking for food. However, the way they do this causes a lot of problems for people. Some of them ruin crops. Some lay their eggs in our food cupboards. Some pests are just annoying, but others can be deadly.

An Annoying Arachnid

Perhaps after spending time outside, you've discovered you have lots of extremely itchy, small red bites. You didn't see any bugs. What happened?

Bugs called chiggers may be to blame. These seemingly invisible creatures are only about 0.016 inch (0.4 mm) long. If you viewed one through a microscope, you would think it was an insect since it has six legs. However, a chigger is really a mite in its larval stage. When it's grown, it will have eight legs like all arachnids, and it will feed mostly on plants.

Chiggers are red, but not because they suck blood. They

Fast Fact

Some people believe that chiggers bury themselves in your skin. However, this isn't true. Hot water and soap is typically enough to wash chiggers and their larvae off.

A chigger's mouthparts are nearly impossible to see without a microscope.

use their short, delicate mouthparts to pierce areas of thin skin. A chemical in their saliva dissolves skin cells, and they drink the liquid. If the person doesn't knock the chigger off their body, it will continue to feed for three or four days!

Bugs for Breakfast?

Next time you have breakfast, you might discover you're not the only one who thought cereal sounded good. Numerous beetles and other insects feed on food products you might have at home.

Saw-toothed grain beetles, red flour beetles, and confused flour beetles are slender, flat, and dark red or brown. All feed on cereals, grains, and dried fruit. Saw-toothed grain beetles have a sweet tooth and will also snack on your candy.

Drugstore beetles are covered with small hairs. Their head is tucked down below the front of their body and can't be seen from above. In addition to grains and cereals, they eat spices, makeup, medicines, and even the poison strychnine! All these beetles are about 0.1 inch (2.5 mm) long.

Pantry moths are another kind of bug that lay their eggs in food. Once they're in a cupboard, it takes a lot of work to get rid of them for good.

SAVE THE BEES

Scientists first found *Varroa* mites in the United States in 1987. Adult female *Varroa* mites are shiny, reddish brown, shield shaped, and about 0.04 inch (1 mm) long and 0.06 inch (1.5 mm) wide. Males are about half that size.

Varroa mites feed on both adult honeybees and larvae. They pierce the insect's body, then suck out the juices. If all the honeybees in the world died, our diet would change greatly. Honeybees give us more than honey. Many of the fruits and vegetables we eat wouldn't exist without the **pollination** carried out by honeybees. That's why beekeepers are working on ways to fight *Varroa* mites.

Kitchen Pests

Almost everyone has seen fruit flies in their kitchen. These tiny insects are about 0.125 inch (3 mm) long and usually have red eyes. They breed on ripe fruits and vegetables that aren't refrigerated, but they also breed in places you might not expect—drains, empty bottles and cans, trash containers, and even mops and cleaning rags! They're mostly just annoying, but they can spread bacteria.

Fast Fact

One way people get rid of fruit flies is by putting apple cider vinegar in a cup along with some warm water and dish soap. The soap makes it impossible for the flies to stay on the surface of the liquid, so they drown.

Up close, it's possible to see
the color of a fruit fly's eyes.

POLLINATION

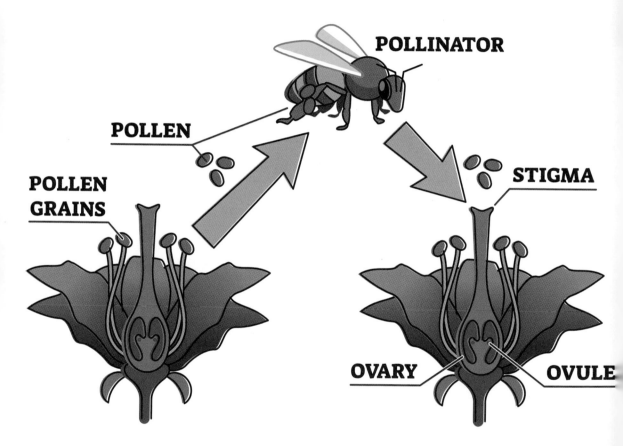

This diagram shows how pollination works.

Chapter Four

HELPFUL CRITTERS

Some bugs can be helpful to people. For example, pollinators help us by making sure our crops grow. Worldwide, about 75 percent of the crops humans grow wouldn't produce food without pollinators.

In some cases, bugs can be both helpful and annoying! For example, if you've ever had a picnic, you've probably had to swat flies away from your food. However, some flies are pollinators, and some are part of certain fishes' diet. If every fly disappeared from the Earth, our picnics would be more peaceful, but we might not have anything to eat at them!

Fast Fact

Some bugs help keep water clean. For example, whirligig beetles swim in waterways and clean them by eating dead or dying insects and debris.

Dust Mites

You may not realize it, but your bed is a crowded place. It's home to tens of thousands—maybe millions—of dust mites. These little arachnids eat the skin flakes that people and their pets shed constantly. In fact, their scientific name is *Dermatophagoides*, which means "skin eater."

Bugs are an important part of food webs. If they all died, so would other animals.

Dust mites are really tiny—just 0.01 inch (0.25 mm) long. They have long **setae** along the edges of their body. Short setae cover the rest of the body and the legs. They have no eyes or antennae. They have no real head, either—just a group of mouthparts. They're among

Fast Fact

Dust mites are helpful, but they can be harmful sometimes too. They're a main source of allergies because they can leave up to 100,000 of their waste particles in 0.03 ounce (0.85 grams) of dust.

Under a microscope, it's possible to see what a dust mite looks like.

the creepiest-looking tiny bugs out there, but they're useful. Imagine the thick layer of skin flakes that would cover everything if it weren't for dust mites!

Ladybugs and Minute Pirate Bugs

Ladybugs, or ladybird beetles, and minute pirate bugs are predators of plant-eating pests. Almost everyone is familiar with ladybugs. These little creatures mainly eat aphids, insects that are about 0.125 inch (3 mm)

TINY ASSASSINS

Assassin spiders are tiny arachnids. They're only about 0.08 inch (2 mm) long—about the size of a grain of rice—but they can be deadly for other spiders. Assassin spiders stab their prey with **venom**-filled fangs located at the end of extremely long jaws. To support these long jaws, the spiders have developed a very long neck. For this reason, they're sometimes called pelican spiders.

In 1854, scientists discovered assassin spider fossils frozen in 50-million-year-old amber. It wasn't until years later that they realized these little bugs are still around today! They live mostly in Madagascar, South Africa, and Australia.

long and have mouthparts designed to pierce plants and suck out juices. Most adult aphids are wingless. Their hind end bears two short tubes called cornicles that put out a liquid likely used for defense. Aphids can be harmful to plants, but ladybugs aren't, so the ladybugs help save our food by eating aphids. This might be why some people think seeing a ladybug is a sign of good luck!

Farmers also like minute pirate bugs because they eat insects that

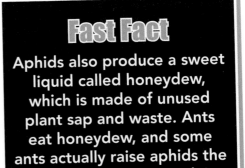

Fast Fact

Aphids also produce a sweet liquid called honeydew, which is made of unused plant sap and waste. Ants eat honeydew, and some ants actually raise aphids the way people raise cattle!

feed on corn, potatoes, and other crops. The bugs dine on spider mites, which damage many garden vegetables, fruits, and flowers and harm some trees. Because minute pirate bugs are so good at getting rid of so many pests, people sometimes buy them to put among their crops or in their gardens. Unfortunately, in late summer, they can become minor pests themselves—they start biting people!

Whether they're helpful, harmful, or somewhere in between, bugs are here to stay! Learning more about them, including by studying them under microscopes, helps us make informed choices about what to do when we encounter them.

Minute pirate bugs are true bugs.

1. What traits do you think a bug would have to have to survive in extreme heat or cold?

2. What are the benefits of compound eyes?

3. What are some other bugs that are both helpful and annoying?

4. What bugs would you most like to look at under a microscope?

assassin: Someone or something that kills with a sudden attack.

exoskeleton: The hard outer covering of an animal's body.

fascinating: Extremely interesting.

forewing: Either of the front wings of a four-winged insect.

membrane: A thin, soft, flexible sheet or layer, especially of a plant or animal part.

parasitic: Living in or on another organism, usually causing it harm.

pollination: A process in which pollen is transferred between plants to create fruits, vegetables, and flowers.

setae: A thin, stiff, hairlike organ on some animals and plants (singular: seta).

stagnant: Not flowing in a current or stream.

venom: Poison produced by some animals and passed to a victim usually by biting or stinging.

FIND OUT MORE

Books

Boone, Mary. *Bugs for Breakfast: How Eating Insects Could Help Save the Planet*. Chicago, IL: Chicago Review Press, 2022.

Hickman, Pamela. *Bugs*. Toronto, ON: Kids Can Press, 2019.

Kurlansky, Mark, and Jia Liu. *Bugs in Danger: Our Vanishing Bees, Butterflies, and Beetles*. New York, NY: Bloomsbury Children's Books, 2019.

Websites

BrainPop: Arachnids
www.brainpop.com/science/diversityoflife/arachnids
Watch a movie and play a game to find out about arachnids.

The Bug Club
www.amentsoc.org/bug-club
Play games, do activities, and learn facts about all kinds of bugs.

Insect Identification
www.insectidentification.org
Have you seen a bug that you can't identify? Try to find it here.

INDEX